King Kamehameha I

Published and Distributed by
HAWAIIAN SERVICE, INC.
P.O. Box 2835
Honolulu, Hawaii 96803

*Cover Illustration: Tiki God of Kukailimoku

Let's
Learn
A
Little
Hawaiian

ISBN 0-930492-07-2

Table
of Contents

Now, let's learn a little about the Hawaiian Language...

It is a dialect of the Polynesian tongue, other variations of which are spoken by Samoans, Tahitians, Marquesans, Tuamotuans and Maoris.

The Hawaiian alphabet has only 12 letters:
The vowels are the same as in English, A, E, I, O, U. The consonants are limited to H, K, L, M, N, P and W.

The vowels are pronounced:
A as in father, E as in vein, I as "ee" in peep, O as in own, and U as "oo" in boo.

The consonants are pronounced:
H as in hale, K as in Kate, L as in laid, M as in moon, N as in noon, P as in peak, and W as in always.

Four primary rules to follow:
1. Every word must end in a vowel.
2. Every consonant must be followed by at least one vowel.
3. Every syllable must end in a vowel.
4. Divide into syllables for easy pronunciation: Ka/la/ni/a/na/o/le.

Popular expressions you'll want to remember:

ALOHA...means "hello, goodbye, love, here's how" (as a toast).

ALOHA KAKAHIAKA..."Good morning."

ALOHA AHIAHI..."Good evening."

ALOHA KAKOU..."Greetings, everybody."

OKOLE MALUNA..."Bottoms up!"

PEHEA OE..."How are you?"

MAIKAI..."Fine."

MAHALO NUI..."Thanks a lot."

KIPA MAI..."You're welcome."

HAUOLI LA HANAU..."Happy Birthday."

MELE KALIKIMAKA..."Merry Christmas."

HAUOLI MAKAHIKI HOU..."Happy New Year!"

PAU..."Finished."

Boy's Names

A

Aaron—**Aalona**
Abel—**Apela**
Abner—**Apenela**
Abraham—**Apelehama**
Adam—**Akamu**
Albert—**Alapaki**
Alexander—**Alekanekelo**
Alfred—**Alapai**
Alton—**Alakona**
Amos—**Amoka**
Andrew—**Anolu**
Anthony—**Akoni**
Archibald—**Aki or Akipala**
Arthur—**Aka**
Austin—**Aukaina**
Augustus—**Aukake**

B

Baldwin—**Polowina**
Barney—**Pane**
Bartholomew—**Pakolomio**
Benjamin—**Peniamina**

Barnabas—**Palenapa**
Bert—**Peka**
Blaine—**Palene**

C

Caesar—**Kaikala**
Caleb—**Kalepa**
Calvin—**Kalawina**
Carl—**Kalela or Kala**
Cecil—**Kikila**
Cephas—**Kepa**
Charles—**Kale**
Christian—**Kalikiano**
Claude—**Kalaukio**
Clement—**Kelemeneke**
Cleveland—**Kelewelana**
Clifton—**Kalipekona**
Cornelius—**Kolenelio**
Cyrus—**Kila**

D

Dan—**Kana**
Daniel—**Kaniela**
David—**Kawika**
Donald—**Konala**

E

Edgar—**Eka**
Edmund—**Ekemana; Ailuene**
Edward—**Aikue; Ailuene**
Edwin—**Ailuene**
Eli—**Eli**
Elias—**Elikai**
Elijah—**Elia**
Elmer—**Elama**
Ernest—**Eneki**
Eugene—**Ailukini**
Ezra—**Ekela**

F

Ferdinand—**Pelekina**
Francis—**Palani**
Frank—**Palani**
Frederick—**Pelelika**

G

Gabriel—**Kapeliela**
George—**Keoki**

Gerald—**Kelala**
Gideon—**Kikiona**
Gilbert—**Kilipaki**
Gordon—**Kokona**

H

Harold—**Hale**
Harry—**Hale**
Harvey—**Halewe**
Henry—**Heneli**
Herbert—**Hapaki**
Herman—**Helemana**
Hiram—**Hailama**
Homer—**Homela**
Horace—**Holeka**
Howard—**Hoaka**
Hugh—**Huko**
Hugo—**Huko**

I

Issac—**Aikake or Ikaaka**
Israel—**Ikelaela**

J

Jack—**Keaka**
Jacob—**Iakopa**

James—**Kimo**
Jay—**Ke**
Jeremiah—**Ielemia**
Jerry—**Kele**
Jesse—**Ieke**
Jimmy—**Kime**
Joel—**Ioela**
Jonah—**Iona**
Jonathan—**Kiakona**
Joseph—**Iokepa**
Joshua—**Iwikua**
Judah—**Iuka**
Julian—**Kioula**
Julius—**Kioula**

K

Kenneth—**Kanaina**

L

Lawrence—**Lowena**
Laurence—**Lowena**
Leonard—**Leonala**
Leopold—**Leopolo**
Levi—**Lewi**
Lewis—**Lui**
Loren—**Lolena**
Louis—**Lui**
Lorrin—**Lolena**

Luke—**Luka**
Luther—**Lukela**
Lota—**Loka**

M

Manuel—**Manuela**
Mark—**Maleko**
Martin—**Makini**
Matthew—**Makaio**
Moses—**Moke**
Micah—**Maika**
Maximilian—**Makimilio**

N

Nathan—**Kamakana**
Nathaniel—**Nakaniela**
Nicholas—**Nikolo**
Noah—**Noa**
Noel—**Noela**

O

Ollie—**Ole**
Oliver—**Oliwa**

Oscar—**Oka**
Owen—**Owene**

P

Paul—**Paulo**
Peter—**Pekelo; (Pika)**
Philip—**Pilipo**
Preston—**Pelekekona**

R

Ralph—**Lalapa**
Raphael—**Lapaela**
Raymond—**Lemona**
Reuben—**Lupine**
Rex—**Leke**
Richard—**Likeke**
Robert—**Lopaka**
Roger—**Lokeke**
Roy—**Loe**
Rufus—**Lupeka**

S

Samson—**Kamekona**
Samuel—**Kamuela**

Seth—**Kepa**
Saul—**Kaulo**
Silas—**Kila**
Simeon—**Kimeona**
Simon—**Kimona**
Solomon—**Kolomona**
Stephen—**Kinoini**

T

Thaddeus—**Kakina**
Theodore—**Keohokalole**
Thomas—**Koma or Kamaki**
Titus—**Kiko**
Tommy—**Kome**

W

Wayne—**Wene**
Walter—**Walaka**
William—**Wiliama**

Girl's Names

A

Abigail—**Apikaila**
Adeline—**Akalina**
Alice—**Alika**
Almira—**Alamila**
Amelia—**Amalia**
Amy—**Ema**
Anna—**Ana**
Anne—**Ane**
Ann—**Ana; Ane**

B

Barbara—**Papela**
Beatrice—**Piakalike**
Bertha—**Peke**
Bessie—**Pakake**
Blanche—**Palaneke**

C

Carmen—**Kamene**
Caroline—**Kalolina**

Catherine—**Kakalina**
Cecilia—**Kikilia**
Charlene—**Kaleene**
Charlotte—**Kaloka**
Christina—**Kilikina**
Clara—**Kalala**
Cora—**Kalohi**
Cornelia—**Kolenelia**

D

Daisy—**Kaiki**
Delia—**Kilia**
Delma—**Kelema**
Diana—**Kina**
Dinah—**Kina**
Dora—**Kalohi**
Doris—**Kolika**
Dorothy—**Koleka**
Deborah—**Kepola**

E

Edith—**Ikaika**
Edna—**Ekena**
Eleanor—**Elinala**
Elizabeth—**Elikapeka**
Eliza—**Ilaika**

Ella—**Ela**
Ellen—**Elena**
Elsie—**Eleke**
Elvira—**Elewaila**
Emily—**Emelia**
Emma—**Ema**
Esther—**Ekekela**
Ethel—**Ekela**
Eunice—**Uneka**
Eva—**Ewa**
Evangeline—**Euanelia**
Eveline—**Ewalina**

F

Fanny—**Pane**
Frances—**Pane**
Flora—**Palola**
Florence—**Pololena**

G

Gertrude—**Kelekulu**
Georgiana—**Keokiana**
Gail—**Kaila**
Georgia—**Keokia**
Georgina—**Keokina**
Glendine—**Kelenakina**
Genevieve—**Kenewiwe**
Grace—**Kaleki**

DONNA - KONA
Ken - Kena
Carol - Kalola
Judy - IUKi

2.60
1.0

fic **G**rain **L**td.

◦—◦‖◦—◦

630
190
440

RKETING SERVICE

R

AND RAPE SEED

TORS OF

CALS AND FERTILIZERS

◦—◦‖◦—◦

e : **Calgary**

Edmonton, Vancouver

H

Hannah—**Hana**
Harriet—**Haliaka**
Hazel—**Hekela**
Helen—**Helena**
Helena—**Helena**
Henrietta—**Heneliaka**
Hester—**Kekala**

I

Ida—**Aika**
Irene—**Ailine**
Irma—**Ema**
Isabel—**Ikapela (or Elikapeka)**
  (same as Elizabeth)

J

Jane—**Kina**
Jaunita—**Wanika**
Jeannette—**Kina**
Josephine—**Kepina**
Julia—**Kulia**
Juliet—**Kulia**

K

Kate—**Keke**
Kay—**Ke**
Kathleen—**Kakeline**

L

Laura—**Lala**
Leonora—**Leonala**
Lena—**Lina**
Lillian—**Liliana**
Lily—**Lilia**
Lois—**Loika**
Lola—**Lola**
Louise—**Luika**
Lucy—**Luika**
Lydia—**Lilia**

M

Mabel—**Mepala**
Madeline—**Makalena**
Margaret—**Makaleka**
Maria—**Malaea**
Marion—**Meleana**
Martha—**Maleka**
Mary—**Mele**

May—**Mei; Mahina**
Melvina—**Melewaina**
Mildred—**Mileka**
Minnie—**Mine**
Miriam—**Miliama**
Muriel—**Muliela**

N

Nancy—**Ane**
Nellie—**Nele**
Nora—**Nola**
Norma—**Noma**

O

Olive—**Oliwia**

P

Pauline—**Polina**
Pearl—**(Momi) Pele**
Phebe—**Poipe**
Polly—**Poli**
Pricilla—**Pelekila**

R

Rachel—**Lahela**
Rebecca—**Lepeka**

Rhoda—**Loka**
Rose—**Loke**
Rosalie—**Lokalia**
Ruby—**(Momi) Lupe**
Ruth—**Luka**

S

Sally—**Kale**
Sarah—**Kela**
Shirley—**Kele**
Sophia—**Kopaia**
Stella—**Kekela**
Susan—**Kukana**

T

Thelma—**Kelemia**
Theresa—**Kelika**

V

Victoria—**Wikolia**
Violet—**Wioleka**
Virginia—**Wilikina**
Vivian—**Wiwiana**

Over 2,000
English to Hawaiian words

a—he; ke
abdomen—opu
abide—e noho iki
ablaze—aa i ke ahi
able—hiki
abolish—e hoopau
about—aneane; kokoke
above—maluna ae; oi ae
abrupt—kalakala
absent—hiki ole mai
absolute—ma na ano a pau
accept—apono; hooia
accident—ulia
accompany—hele pu
accomplish—loaa ka holopono
according—alika ia
account—kuleana
acquaintance—kamaaina; hoalauna
accustom—maamau
acre—eka
across—maua'e
act—hana; ano
action—ano; hana;
active—oni mau
actual—pololei; oiaio; hooko pono
add—houluulu
addition—houluulu
address—wahi noho
admit—aeia
admire—makahehi; hoohihi
advance—haawi-mua; uku-mua
advantage—holopono
advice—olelo a'o

23

advise—olelo kauoha
affect—loaa ia haawina hookahi
afraid—hopohopo; maka'u
after—mahope
afternoon—auinala
afterward—mahope aku
again—hou
against—kue
age—makahiki
ago—manawa loihi hala; li'u wale
agree—aelike
agriculture—na mea ulu
ah—kahaha
aid—kokua
aim—pololei; kaulona
air—ea
alarm—hikilele; hoopuiwa
alcohol—wai kulu
alike—ua like
alive—ola
all—apau
allow—ae; hoapono
almost—aneane loa; kokoke loa
alone—oia hookahi
along—pu; hele pu
aloud—leo nui
already—makaukau
also—pela no hoi
although—eia nae
always—mau hana mau; i na wa apau
am—wau
America—Amelika
American—Kanaka Amelika
among—iloko o ia; iwaena o ia
amount—huina
an—pilikahi
ancient—kahiko

and—ame
anger—inaina
angel—anela
animal—holoholona
another—kekahi mea okoa
answer—haina
anxious—pihoihoi; ake nui
any—kekahi ano; ke kau wahi
anything—mea like ole; ano like ole
apart—hookaawale
appeal—hoopii
appear—hoopuka; puka ae; ike ia ae
appearance—hiki ana aku
applaud—e mahalo
apple—apala
apply—hoopilipu
appoint—hookohu; koho
approach—hiki aku; hoea
approve—hooia
arch—pi'o
are—wale no; he
area—laula o ka aina
arise—e ku ae
arm—lima
armor—kapakila
army—puali
arose—ala
around—apuni
arrange—hoomakaukau
arrest—e hopu
arrive—ku mai
arrow—ihe; pua-kaka
art—loina
article—pauku; kekahi apana
as—ma (me); me he la
ascend—e pii ana
ashamed—hilahila

aside—ma ka aoao; pili aoao
ask—ninau; noi
asleep—ua hiamoe
assembly—anaina
assist—kokua
assure—hoopaa
at—ma
ate—ua ai
attack—paio aku; kue aku
attempt—e hoao
attend—hiki aku; maiama; lawelawe
attention—hoolohe; makaukau
aunt—makuahine pilikama
author—mea haku
authority—leo mana; poo; ma ke kauoha
autumn—kau kupulau
avenue—alahele; alanui
avoid—e alo ae
await—kakali
awake—puoho; ala
away—kahi e; wahi okoa
awful—ilihia; weliweli
ax (axe)—ko'i
axel—paipaikomo
aye—ae

B

baboon—keho nui
baby—pepe
back—kua
bad—inoino

bade—kauoha
bag—paiki; eke
bail—pela
bake—hoomo'a oma
balance—koena
bald—ohule; niania
ball—kinipopo
band—pana
bank—panako
bare—waiho wale
bark—ili laau
barn—hale waiho ukana
barrel—pahu
base—kahua
basket—hina'i
bath—auau
bathe—e auau
battle—hooili kaua
bay—lokia; kai kuono
be—e pono
beach—aekai; kahakai
beam—kaola
bean—huaai pi
bear—pea
beard—umiumi
beast—holoholona
beat—paluku; apuhi
beautiful—nani; u'i
beauty—u'i
became—lilo ana ae
because—no ka mea
become—lilo ae la
bed—wahi moe
bee—meli
been—aku nei
beer—mea inu
before—mamua

27

beg—nonoi
began—hoomaka
beggar—makilo; nonoi
begin—hoomaka
begun—hoomaka
behind—mahope
behold—aia hoi
being—a no ka mea; ma ke ano
believe—hilinai
believe—hilina'i; manaoi'o
bell—pele
belly—opu
belong—nolaila
below—malalo
belt—kaula apo
bench—noho laau
beneath—malalo ae
benefit—pomaikai
bend—kulou; hoopi'o
bent—kapakahi; kulou
berry—he huaai
beside—eia nae; ma kekahi; ano
best—oi; helu ekahi
better—pono iki
between—mawaena
beyond—ma o aku
bid—kauoha; koho
big—nui
bind—hoopaa
bird—manu
birthday—la hanau
birth—hanau
bit—he wahi apana iki; kekahi wahi
bite—nahu
bitter—awahia; mulea
black—eleele

blacksmith—amala
blade—kila
blame—hoahewa
blank—pepa i kakau ole ia
blaze—e a ana
bleach—hookeokeo
bless—hoopomaikai
blessing—hoopomaikai ana
blew—puhi; puhia
blind—makapo
block—apana; mahele; ake'ake'a
blood—koko
bloom—mohala; opuu
blossom—mohala; (pua opuu)
blow—puupuu
blue—polu; uliuli
board—papa
boast—kaena
boat—waapa
body—kino
boil—paila
bold—nahoa
bolt—he laka hoopaa
bond—pona
bone—iwi
boot—kamaa puki
border—ka'e; palena
bore—paeli
borrow—e noi
bosom—poli
bottle—omole
bottom—papaku
book—puke
born—hanau
both—laua elua
bough—he lala i ulunui ia me ka lau
bought—kuai

bound—kupahu; owiliia
bow—kulou; o mua o ka waa
bowl—pola
box—pahu
boy—keikikane
brain—lolo
brake—peleki
branch—lala
brass—keleawe
brave—koa; wiwo ole
bread—palaoa
break—uhaki; uha'i
breakfast—ai'na kakahiaka
breast—umauma
breathe—hanu; aho
breeze—koaniani makani; aheahe makani
brick—pohaku uinihapa
bride—wahine e male ana
bridge—uwapo
brief—hoopokole
bright—naauao; makaukau; malamalama
bring—lawe mai
broad—akea
broke—haki
brook—kahawai liilii
brother—kaikunane; (hoahanau kane)
brought—lawe mai
brow—kuemaka
brown—haeleele
brush—palaki
bubble—hu'a kopa
bud—opuu
build—kukulu; hooulu
building—hale
bull—na holoholona kane
bunch—ahui
bundle—puolo

burden—haawe kaumaha
burn—puhi; ho-a
burst—pa-hu
bury—kanu
bush—opuu nahelehele
bushel—pukela
business—oihana
busy—paa mau ka manawa; hana mau
but—aka
butcher—he mea okioki i'o holoholona
butter—waiupaka
buttock—okole
buxom—onaona
buy—kuai
by—ma ka
buzz—kamumumu

C

cabbage—kapika
cactus—panini
cake—meaono
calendar—alemanaka
California—Kaleponi
call—kahea; kipa; launa
calm—lai
calm—la'i; hala'i
came—hiki mai
camp—hoomoana
can—hiki; kini
canal—auwai; auwaha
candle—ihoiho

candy—kana-ke
cannot—aole hiki
canoe—waa
cap—papale kapu
cape—he lole aahu; kuka; he lae aina
captain—kapena
car—kaa
card—pepa mano'ano'a
care—malama pono
careful—akahele
carpenter—kamana
carriage—kaa
carry—hapai
cart—kaa
carve—kalai
case—pahu; pahu wa-hi
cast—e kiola; hoolei; hoohehee
castle—kakela
cat—popoki
catch—hopu
cattle—holoholona; pipi
caught—loaa; paa
cause—kumu; no ke kumu
cave—a-na
cease—hooki; hoopau
celebrate—hoohiwahiwa; hoomanao
cell—keena liilii
cellar—ka lua malalo ae o ka hale
cent—keneka
center—kikowaena
central—kikowaena
century—kenekuria
certain—kekahi ano
chair—noho
chamber—rumi moe; he apo e paa ai ka poka
chance—manawa kupono
change—hoololi; loli

chap—hoaloha; kokoolua; aikane
chapel—luakini
character—ke ano; kulana;
charge—kaki; auhauia
charity—manawalea
charm—ohuohu; hiwahiwa
chase—uhai
cheap—emi
check—oki; hookaawale
cheek—papalina
cheer—hoole'a aku; hoohauoli
cheerful—hoohauoli; ohaoha
cheese—waiupaka paa
cherry—waihooluu haula
chest—umauma
chicken—moa
chief—poo (ma ka oihana)
child—keiki
children—kamalii
chill—maeele
chimney—puka uwahi
China—Kina

choice—mea ano nui; helu ekahi
choose—e kohokoho
chop—pokepoke
chose (n)—kohoia
Christian—Kalikiano
Christmas—Kalikimaka
church—halepule
circle—a-na poepoe
circumstance—ka mea; ke ano; ke kulana
citizen—makaainana
city—kulanakauhale
civil—kiwila
claim—koi; kuleana
clasp—e apo; kuapo
class—papakula

clay—lepo palolo
clean—maemae
clear—malaelae
clerk—kakauolelo
cliff—niao pali
climate—na wa o ke kau
climb—pii; panana
clock—uwaki
close—pani; hahana
cloth—lole; aahu
clothes—na lole
cloud—ao; opua
club—kalapu; ahahui
coach—kumua'o
coal—nanahu
coarse—kalakala
coast—kahakai; holopiliaina
coat—kuka; (lole aahu)
cock—moa kane
coffee—kope
coin—kala
cold—anuanu; hu'ihu'i
collar—aikala
collect—ohi
college—halekula kiekie
color—waihooluu
colony—panalaau
colt—lio keiki
column—kolamu
combine—hoohui; i huiia
come—hele mai
comfort—oluolu; maha
comfortable—oluolu
coming—e hiki mai ana
command—kauoha
commerce—kalepa waiwai
common—mea mau; ike mau ia

companion—hoa; hoahele; hoalauna
company—hui; ahahaui
compare—hoohalikelike
compass—panana
compel—kauohaia e hana aku pela; mana kauoha
complain—ohumu; hoohalahala
complete—pau pono
conceal—hunakele; huna
concern—e pili ana
conclude—ka hopena; e huipu ana
condemn—ua ahewaia
condition—kulana
conduct—hookele
confess—mihi; e mihi ana
congress—hale kaukanawai o Amelika
connect—hoohui; hui
conquer—lanakila
conscience—lunaikehala
consent—apono; ae
consist—huipu
contain—e pili ana
continent—mahele aina nui
continue—hoomauia
contract—aelike; kuikahi pu
contrary—kue; maka aoao kue
control—hoomalu
convenient—me ka hiki; mea hiki
conversation—kukakuka kamailio
cook—kuke
cool—oluolu; hu'ihu'i
copper—keleawe
copy—kope
cord—kaula; paila wahie
corn—kulina
corner—kihi
correct—pololei
cost—kumukuai

costly—nui ka lilo; hoolilo
cottage—pahale
cotton—hulu hipa
couch—punee
could—hiki
council—ahakuka
counsel—loio
count—helu
country—aina; kuaaina
county—kalana
couple—palua
courage—wiwo ole; aa; manao wiwo ole
course—alahele; he au; wa
court—aha hookolokolo
cousin—hoahanau
cover—ke pani; po'i umoki
cow—pipi wahine
cozy—oluolu
crack—owa; nakakaka
crazy—pupule
cream—hau-kilima
create—hookumu
creature—na mea kino me ka hanu ola
credit—hilinai; manao hoopono
crew—luina
creep—nee
cried—ua uwe
crime—kalaima
crop—ke kau oo o na mea kanu
cross—huhu; ke'e
crow—kani ana a ka moakane
cruel—lokoino
crush—opa-pu
cry—uwe
cultivate—mahiai; e paka i ka leo
cunning—maalea; piha eu
cup—kiaha

cure—hoola
curious—ano e; mahaoi
curl—mimilo
current—ke au
curse—kuamuamu
curtain—paku
custom—maa mau
cut—oki
cycle—wa

D

daily—hana mau
dam—kumulau
damage—poho; poino
daily—hana mau; (kela ame keia manawa)
dance—hula
danger—ulia
dangerous—popilikia
dare—aa; manao hopo ole
dark—poeleele
darkness—pouliuli
darling—ipo
dart—anapu
dash—popo'i; paki
date—manawa; ka la; wa
daughter—kaikamahine
dawn—wehe'na kaiao
day—la
dead—make
deal—kekahi hana e noonoo ia ana
dear—mea-aloha

death—make
debt—aie
decay—popopo
deceive—apuhi; hoopunipuni
decide—apono
decent—kupono; kohupono
deck—oneki;
declare—kukala
decline—hoole; iho'na
deed—palapala hoolilo
deep—hohonu
deer—kia
defend—kupale; kokua; hoopakele
defense—kupale
defraud—apuka
degree—kekele
delay—hoomoe-iki
delicate—palupalu
delight—ma-ma; hauoli
deliver—haawi aku; lawe aku e haawi
demand—koi
den—hale-lua
deny—hoole
depart—kaawale; e holo ana
department—keena oihana
depend—kauka'i
depth—hohonu
descend—e iho; iho'na
describe—hoike ana; hoakaka
desert—kula panoa
deserve—e pono
design—he a-na lole; he a-na i kaha ia
desire—iini; ake
desk—pakaukau
despair—poho ka manaolana
despise—hoowahawaha
destroy—hoinoino; e hoolei

destruction—lukuia
determine—e noonoo ana e hana
develop—e hoomohala i ka noonoo
devil—kepolo
devote—pina'i; haawi pau
dew—kehau
diamond—kaimana
did—i hana
didn't—aole
die—ua make
difference—ano-e
different—ano-e; kuee
difficult—ano paakiki; pohihihi
dig—eli; paeli
dim—pohina
dine—ai
dinner—ai'na; paina
dip—kio'e
direct—pololei
direction—alahele
disappear—nalowale; nalohia
discover—ua loaa
discovery—ka loaa mua
disease—he ma'i
dish—pa; ipukai
display—hoikeike
dispose—e hoolilo aku
dispute—hoopaapaa
distance—mamao
distant—mamao
distinct—moakaka
distress—hoehaeha
district—apana; mahele
disturb—hoohaunaele; hoopilikia; hoouluhua
ditch—auwai; auwaha
divide—mahele; kekahi aoao o ke awawa
divine—ke Mea Kiekie

do—hana
doctor—kauka
does—hana
dog—ilio
doll—kii; mea paani a na keiki
dollar—kala
domestic—pili ohana o ka home; kuloko
done—hana
don't—mai; hiki ole
door—puka
dot—kiko
double—palua
doubt—kanalua
dove—manu nunu
down—ilalo
doze—kulihiamoe
dozen—hookahi kakini
drain—hookahekahe
drawer—unuhi; pahu-ume
dread—hopohopo
dreadful—piha i ka hopohopo
draft—pepa kikoo dala; pa ana o ka makani
  ma ka hakahaka
drag—kaualako
dream—moeuhane
dress—lole aahu; ho-aahu
drink—inu
drip—kulu
drew—unuhi; wehe mai
drill—paikau; he mea wili
drive—kalaiwa
droop—kukule; mae
drop—haule
drove—ho-a pu-a; kaiehu
drown—piholo
drum—pahu
dry—maloo

duck—kaka
dull—pau ka oi; kumumu
dumb—mumule
dung—kukae
during—ia wa; ia manawa
dust—lepo
duty—hana
dwell—i noho mau ai; kahi noho
dying—aneane make

E

each—pakahi
eager—akenui; iini
eagle—aeko
ear—pepeiao
early—hiki mua; wanaao kakahiaka nui
earn—hualoaa; ka hua i loaa mai
earnest—ikaika ma ka manao
earth—honua
ease—maha; olu
easily—hiki wale no
east—hikina
eastern—aoao hikina
easy—hiki wale; mama-pu
eat—ai
echo—kupina'i
edge—ka'e; lihi; niao
education—hoonaauao
eel—puhi
effect—hopena mai
effort—hoao; manao nui; noonoo nui
egg—hua; huamoa; hua-kaka

eight—ewalu
eighteen—umikumamawalu
eighth—papa ewalu; he ewalu
either—kekahi o ia
elate—hoopihoihoi
elect—e koho
election—koho ana
electric—uwila
eleven—umikumamakahi
else—kekahi mea okoa aku
embrace—apo; puili
emotion—pihoihoi
emperor—emepela
empire—emepaea
employ—ninini a pau; hakahaka
encourage—hoohoihoi; hoolana manao
end—hopena
endure—ahonui; hoomanawanui
enemy—enemi
engage—hoopalau; hoolimalima
engine—enekini
enjoy—olioli
enormous—nui hewahewa
enough—lawa
enter—komo
entertain—hoolaule'a
entire—holookoa
entrance—wahi komo; puka komo
envy—lili; huwa
equal—kaulike
ere—mamua aku nei
erect—ku pololei; kukulu a pololei; kukulu
error—hewa; pahemahema
escape—holomahuka
especial—oiai hoi
establish—kukulu ana
estate—waiwai paa

eternal—mai kinohi a mau loa aku
even—pela i'o; kulike; laumania
evening—ahiahi
event—eia nae; hana nui
ever—kekahi wa; oia mau
every—pau loa
everybody—na poe a pau
everything—na mea a pau
everywhere—na wahi a pau
evil—ino; hewa; poino
exact—like loa
examine—ninaninau ia; huli ana
example—he mea hoomaikeike
exceed—oi wale aku; pakela oi loa
excellent—maikai loa
except—koe nae
exchange—hoololi
excite—pihoihoi
exclaim—kahea leo nui; e hooho
excuse—e hookuu ia; kalaia
expect—upu; ke upu aku nei
expense—hoolilo
experience—ka hoomaopopo ana; ka ike i loaa ma
  ka hana; kona ike iho
explain—hoomoakaka; wehewehe aku
express—kaa ukana; hoike manao
extend—hooloihi
extreme—hope loa
eye—maka
eyelash—lihilihi

F

fable—olelo nane
face—papalina

fact—ke kumu
factory—halehana
fade—mae
fail—hoihope; haulehope
faint—maule
fair—ua pono; kaulike; onaona; hoikeike
fairy—kupua
faith—manaoio
faithful—hoopono; hookopono
fall—haule; hiolo; hina
false—wahahee; hoopunipuni
fame—kaulana
familiar—mea mau; kamaaina ia
family—ohana
famous—kaulana
fan—peahi
fancy—u'i; nani
far—mamao
fare—auhau; uku
farewell—aloha
farmer—kanaka mahiai
farther—loihi aku; i o loa aku
fashion—paikini; ke ano mau
fast—awiwi
fasten—hoopaaia; hauhoaia
fat—momona
fate—hopena; luahi
father—makuakane
fault—hewa
favorite—punahele
fear—hopohopo
fearful—hopohopo
feast—ahaaina
feather—hulu
feature—hiohiona
feed—hanai; ai a na holoholona
feel—noonoo; hoopa-pa

44

feeling—noonoo
feet—wawae
fed—hanai
fell—haule
fellow—hoa; hoalauna; kela kanaka
felt—hoopapa; haha
female—wahine
fence—pa aina
fetch—lawe mai; kii aku a lawe mai
fever—piwa
few—kakaikahi
field—mahinaai; mala
fierce—weliweli
fifteen—umikumamalima
fifty—kanalima
fight—hakaka
figure—huahelu
file—apuapu; laina pololei
fill—hoopiha
final—panina; hopena
finally—oia hoi
find—loaa
fine—hoopa'i; maikai
finger—manamanalima
finish—pau
fire—ahi

firm—paa; kupaa; hui; onipaa
first—mua
fish—i'a
fist—puulima
fit—kupono
five—elima
fix—hana; e hana hou
flag—hae
flame—lapalapa ahi
flash—olapa
flat—palahalaha

45

flatter—hoomalimali
flea—uku lele
fled—ua holo
fleet—ulumoku; mama i ka holo
flesh—i'o
flew—ua lele
flies—lele; nalo
flight—kak lele ana
float—lana; hoolana
flock—pu-a
flood—waikahe
floor—papahele
flour—palaoa maka
flow—kahe
flower—pua
flutter—kapalulu; kapalili
fly—lele
fold—opiopi
folk—ohana
follow—hahai; uhai
following—hahai ana
folly—lapuwale; hupo
fond—punahele
fondle—hooaumoe
food—meaai
foot—wawae
foolish—hupo lalau
for—no
forbid—hookapu
force—ikaika; mana; e lawelawe lima nui
forehead—lae
foreign—olelo e; lahui e
forest—ululaau
forget—poina
forgive—huikala
forgot—poina
forgotten—poinaia

fork—o
form—kulana
former—ka mea mua
fort—papu
forth—imua
fortune—kuonoono
forty—kanaha
forward—hele imua
fought—hakaka; paio
foul—pelapela; haumia
found—loaa
foundation—papahele; kumuhana
fountain—waipua'i
four—eha
fourth—eha; aha
fox—ilio hae
frame—apo
France—Palani
free—lanakila
freedom—kuokoa
freeze—opili
freight—ukana
French—kanaka Palani
frequent—hana mau
fresh—ohaoha; ano hou
fret—hopohopo; ka wa o na meakani
friend—hoaloha
friendly—ano hoaloha
friendship—hoaloha
fright—puiwa
frighten—maka'u; hoopuiwa
from—mai
front—ma ke alo
frost—kehau; ohu
frozen—opili; (i ke anu)
fruit—hua
full—piha

fully—piha pono
fun—le'ale'a; hauoli
funeral—hoolewa
fur—hulu
furnish—hoolawa
furniture—ponohale
further—ma o iki aku
futile—makehewa
future—ia mua aku nei

G

gag—oa
gain—puka
game—he paani
garden—kihapai; mahinaai; mahakea
garment—lole; aahu
gas—ea
gate—hoakoakoa
gate—ipuka pa
gather—hoakoakoa
gave—haawi aku
gay—le'ale'a; olioli
gaze—hakapono
gem—akea; ano nui; na mea apau
generous—akahai; lokomaikai
gentle—oluolu; akahai
gentleman—keonimana
geometry—ano honua
German—Kelemania
Germany—Kelemania
get—kii

giant—kanaka nunui
gift—makana; haawina pomaikai
girl—kaikamahine
give—haawi
given—haawiia
glad—hauoli; hauoli au i ka ike ana ia oe
glance—leha
glass—aniani
glitter—hulalali
globe—poepoe honua
glorious—piha hauoli
glory—kamahao; nani
glove—mikilima
glow—enaena
go—hele
goat—kao
God—Akua
goes—hele

going—e hele ana
gold—kula
golden—he kula
gone—ua hala
good—maikai

goodness—ano maikai
goose—ene
got—loaa
govern—hoomalu
government—aupuni
governor—kiaaina
gown—lole; holoku

gracious—lokomaikai
grade—iliwai; papa
gradual—hoomau; malie; hana malie a hoomau
grain—hunahuna
grand—kiekie; (mea anonui); (nani kamahao)
grandfather—kupunakane

grandmother—kupunawahine kuku
grant—apono; ae; haawi
grape—hua waina
grass—mauu
grateful—hoomaikai
grave—luakupapau
gray—ahinahina; poohina
great—anonui; meanui
green—omaomao
greet—haawi aloha aku
grew—ulu ae
grief—kaumaha; ehaeha
grieve—kaniuhu
grind—hookala; wili
groan—u-hu; na
ground—honua; lepo
group—pu-a-huihui
grove—ululaau
grow—ulu
growth—ulu
guard—makaala; luna kiai
guess—noonoo wale
guest—malihini hookipa
guide—alakai
guilty—ahewaia
gulf—kaikuono
gum—pilali
gun—pu
gut—naau liilii

H

habit—hana maa
had—loaa

hail—ua hekili; e kalahea leo nui
hair—lauoho
half—hapalua
hall—ho-lo
hammer—hamale
hand—lima
handkerchief—hainaka
handle—laau-kano
handsome—u'i nohenohea
hang—li; piliwale
happen—loohia; a loaa wale; me keia
happiness—hauoli
happy—hauoli
harbor—awa kumoku
hard—paakiki
hardly—aole pono loa; hiki kupono ole
harm—pilikia; poino
harness—ili kau-o kaa waiwai ole
harvest—ke kau ohi; (pili i na hea ulu)
has—loaa
hash—haki
haste—awiwi; e au
hasten—awiwi; e auau ka hele'na
hat—papale
hate—hoowahawaha
haul—huki
have—loaa
hay—mauu
he—oia, ia (kane)
head—poo
heal—ola
health—ola kino
heap—puu; hoahu a puu
hear—lohe
heard—lohe
heart—puuwai
heat—wela; mahanahana

heaven—lani
heavy—kaumaha; ko'iko'i
heel—kapuai
height—kiekie
held—paaia
help—kokua
hen—moa wahine
hence—nolaila; eia nae
henceforth—mai keia manawa aku
her—iaia; (wahine)
herd—pu-a holoholona
here—ianei; maanei
hero—wiwo ole; koa
herself—iaia ponoi; nona iho; (wahine)
hid—huna
hide—huna
high—kiekie
hill—puu; pali
him—iaia; (kane)
himself—iaia iho; kona ponoi
hind—na wawae hope
hire—hoolimalima
his—kona
history—moolelo
hit—ku'i e ki a ku
hither—ianei
hog—puaa nui
hold—paa
hole—puka
holiday—la nui
hollow—hakahaka; poho; hohoma
home—home
honest—oiaio; hoopono
honey—wai meli
honor—hanohano
honorable—hanohano
hoof—kapuai wawae holoholona

hook—makau; kilou
hop—kupahu; lele
hope—manaolana
horn—kiwi; ohe
horse—lio
hospital—haukipila
host—haku hale; ona hale
hot—wela
hotel—hokele
hour—hola
house—hale
household—pili home
how—pehea
however—cia nae
howl—uwa
huge—nunui; nui hewahewa
human—ano kanaka
humble—hoohaahaa; akahai
humor—hoonanea
hundred—haneli
hung—liia
hunger—pololi
hungry—pololi
hunt—uhai; uhai holoholona
hunter—kanaka uhai
hurry—awiwi; wikiwiki
hurt—eha
husband—kane
hush—hamau
hut—pupupu hale
hymn—himeni; mele

I

I—owau
ice—hau

idea—noonoo
idiotic—lolo
if—ina
idle—palaualelo
ill—oma'ima'i; nawaliwali
I'll—Na'u
I'm—Owau
image—na helehelena
imagine—manao koho
imbecile—lolo
immediate—ano koke
immortal—ola mau
importance—mea ano nui
important—anonui
impossible—aole e hiki; mea pohihihi
improve—mahuahua; hooi ae
in—iloko
inch—iniha
incline—kulana hi-o; noonoo iho
include—huipu
increase—hoonui
indeed—he oiaio
independent—kuokoa
India—Inia
Indiana—Ilikini
indicate—kuhikuhi
individual—kino hookahi; mea hookahi
industry—oihana oi o ka holomua
influence—mana o ka noonoo
inform—hoike
information—loaa mai ka hoike
injury—poino
ink—inika
inquire—ninau; niele
inside—maloko
instance—emoole; ia manawa koke no
instant—manawa ano; kela manawa koke

instead—ma kahi
instruct—a'o hoonaauao
instruction—ua a'o ia; ua hoonaauaoia
instrument—pila hoolaulea; kekahi mau mea
  paahana
intend—noonoo mua; manao ana; haupu
interest—uku panee
into—iloko; komopono; komo pu iloko
introduce—hoolaha mua; lawe mua mai; ho-
  olauna
invitation—kono
invite—kono
iron—hao
is—oia
island—mokupuni
issue—hoolaha; hua o ka puhaka
it—no
Italian—kanaka Ikalia
Italy—Ikalia (inoa o ke aupuni)
its—oiai
itself—iaia iho
ivory—nihopalaoa

J

jail—hale paahao
jar—ipu lepo; mokuahana
jaw—auwae
jeer—loiloi
jewel—pohaku makamae
job—hana; lopa; (inoa)
join—huipu

joint—huina; hookuina
joke—olelo akaaka
Joseph—Iokepa
journey—kaahele
joy—hauoli
joyful—piha hauoli
judge—lunakanawai
judgment—olelo hooholo
jump—lele
just—kulike
justice—kaulike; hoopono
juvenile—opiopio

K

keel—iwikaele
keep—malama
kept—malama ponoia
kettle—ipu ki
key—ki
kick—pepu
kill—pepehi
kind—ke ano; oluolu
kindly—ano oluolu
kindness—oluolu; akahai
king—moi; alii
kingdom—aupuni
kiss—honi
kitchen—lumi kuke
kitten—popoki keiki
knee—kuli
knew—hoomaopopo; ike no

knife—pahi
knight—naika; kanaka koa
knit—hana lihilihi
knock—kikeke; kulai
knot—nipuu; hipuu
know—ike; hoomaopopo
knowledge—naauao
known—ikeia
knuckle—puupuu lima

L

labor—limahana paahana
lace—lihilihi
lack—alualu; palaka
lad—opio
ladder—alapii
ladies—na leke
lady—leke (wahine i leke)
laid—hoomoe; (waiho wale aku no)
lake—loko nui
lamb—hipa
lame—oopa
lamp—kukui
land—aina
lane—alanui ololi
language—olelo
lap—uha
larceny—aihue
large—nui
lark—laka
last—hope

late—komo hope
latter—ka hope mai o na mea elua
laugh—akaaka
laughter—akaaka
law—kanawai
lawn—he pa i kanu ia i ka mauu
lay—hoomoe; hoomoe pu
lazy—molowa; palaualelo
lead—alakai; kepau
leader—alakai
league—he a-na mile (hookahi liki)
lean—kalele; wiwi
leap—kupahu
learn—a'o
least—apana uuku
leather—ili
leave—waiho; haalele
led—alakai mamua
left—haalele; lima hema
leg—wawae
lend—haawi aku
length—loa
less—emi
lesson—haawina
lest—o
let—hookuu
letter—leka
level—iliwai
levy—hookupu
lewd—haukae
liberty—kuokoa
library—keena malama ia o na puke
lie—hoopunipuni
life—ola
lift—hapai; ka'ika'i
light—malamalama
lightning—uwila

like—makemake
likely—paha
lily—pua lilia
limb—lala
limit—kaupalena
linen—lilina
lion—liona
lip—lehelehe
liquid—mea hee; heehee
list—papahelu
listen—hoolohe
little—uuku
live—kahi noho
lively—cleu
load—piha-ukana; haawe
local—kuloko
locate—huli a loaa; hele e huli
lock—laka
lodge—ahahui malu
log—pauku laau
London—Lakana
lone—oia wale no
lonely—mehameha
long—loihi
look—nana
loose—aluhee; alualu
lord—haku
lose—nalowale; lilo
loss—ua nalowale; ua haule
lost—nalowale
lot—pa; pana; nui
loud—walaau a nui ka leo
love—aloha
lovely—u'i; he nohea
lover—ipo aloha
low—haahaa
lower—malalo iho

59

luck—pomaikai
lumber—papa
lump—puu
luxury—hiwahiwa

M

machine—mikini
mad—huhu
made—hanaia
magic—kamaha'o; pahaohao
magnificent—nani; u'i
maid—wahine kauwa
maiden—wahine i male ole ia
mail—leka
maintain—malama mau
majority—hapanui
make—hana
maker—mea nana i hana
male—kane
manage—e hooponopono
mankind—ke ano kanaka
manner—kulana
manufacture—mea i hana ia e ka lima e mikini paha
many—lehulehu
map—palapala aina
marble—mapala
mark—ma-ka
market—makeke
marriage—male
marry—male
mass—he ahu
mast—kia moku; pahu hae
master—haku
match—kukaepele; paio; hoohalikelike

mate—hoapili; hulipahu
material—mea liilii
matter—kumuhana; mea oa
may—malia; paha
mayor—meia
me—owau
meadow—aina kula i ulu ia e ka mauu
meal—meaai
mean—pi; ka manao
meant—manao; noonoo
measure—a-na
meat—i'o holoholona
medicine—laau lapaau
meet—halawai
melt—hehee
member—hoa hui
memory—hoomanao
men—na kanaka
mend—pahonohono
mention—e ha'i
merchandise—waiwai kalepa
merchant—kanaka kalepa
mercy—ahonui; lokomaikai
mere—wale no; iki
merit—kumu mahalo
message—elele
messenger—elele
met—halawai; hui
method—ano alakai hana
middle—iwaena; kikowaena
midnight—aumoe
midst—waenakonu
might—mana; ikaika; pela paha
mighty—ikaika; mana
mild—aheahe
mile—mile
military—oihana koa
milk—waiu

mill—halewili
million—miliona
mind—noonoo
mine—ka'u
minister—kahunapule
minute—minuke
mirror—aniani kilohi
mist—noe
mistress—wahine poo
mix—hoohuihui
mock—pahenehene
model—he a-na hoohalike
moderate—kaulike
modern—keia wa; ke au hou
modest—akahai
moment—manawa
money—kala
month—mahina
monument—kia hoomanao
moon—mahina
moral—noho'na hoopono; olelo hoonaauao
more—oi aku
morning—kekahiaka
mortal—he aha e make ai; he kanaka
most—hapanui
mother—makuahine
motion—he noi; kuhikuhi e alakai ana
mount—e pii; e ee
mountain—kuahiwi
mourn—kanikau
mouse—iole keiki
mouth—waha
mouthpiece—wahaolelo
move—nee; oni
movement—ka nee ana
mistake—hewa
much—nui; oi
mud—lepo

multiply—hoonui; hoomahuahua
mum—mumule
murder—pepehi kanaka
murmur—nunu olelo; ohumu
music—mele
musical—hookani pila
must—e pono
my—ko'u
myself—ko'u no'u
mystery—pohihihi

N

nab—hopu
nag—lio
nail—kui kakia
naked—holowale
name—inoa
nap—kuluhiamoe
narrow—haiki
nation—lahui
national—pili lahui
native—kanaka
natural—ano mau; oia mau
nature—ano maoli
naughty—kolohe; ino
navy—oihana kaua moana
near—kokoke; aneane
nearly—aneane
neat—maemae; mikioi
necessary—kupono; he mea pono
necessity—akenui
neck—a-i

need—makemake
needle—kui kele
neglect—hoohemahema
negro—nika
neighbor—hoalauna
neither—aole hoi; o kekahi
nest—punana
net—upena
never—aole
new—hou
newspaper—nupepa
New York—Nu loka
next—kekahi aku
nice—maikai; maemae; nani
night—po
nine—eiwa
no—aole
noble(ly)—he alii; mahaloia; hanohano; hoopono
nobody—mea ole; aohe mea
nod—kunou
noise—hauwalaau
none—aole kekahi
noon—awakea
nor—a i ole
nose—ihu
not—aohe; aole
note—he apana pepa hoomanao; pepa kikoo
nothing—aohe; aole; oki loa
notice—hoolaha
novel—kaao
now—keia manawa; ano
nude—ohohelohe
number—helu
numerous—lehulehu; nui loa
nurse—kahu
nut—hua
nutmeg—hua ala

O

oak—oka
oar—hoe waapa
oat—hua-oka;
obey—hoolohe
object—kue; kumuhana
oblige—hoomaikai
observe—malama
obtain—e loaa mai
occasion—wa kupono; manawa kupono
occupy—e noho nei; nohoia
occur—ala mai
ocean—moana
o'clock—manawa o ka hola
odd—paewa; like ole; na helu oi
o'er—maluna ae; ma o ae; kela aoao
of—o
off—hemo; hookuuia; hala aku la
offend—huhu; hoonaukiuki; kue; ehaeha ka noonoo
offense—hana kue kanawai; hana kolohe
offer—haawi; hookupu
office—keena
officer—luna
official—lunanui; poonui
often—pinepine; hana mau
oh—auwe
oil—aila
old—kahiko
olive—oliwa
on—maluna
once—i hookahi; i kekahi
one—hookahi
onion—akaakai
only—wale no
open—wehe
operation—ka hana ia ana; ua lawelawe ia ka hana

opinion—manao
opportunity—wa kupono
oppose—ke'ake'a; aoao kue mai
opposite—kue; kupono mai no kekahi aoao; aoao kue
    or—a i ole
orange—alani
orchard—ululaau hua
order—kauoha
ordinary—maa mau; ano mau
original—noonoo oiaio; o ka mea oiaio mua;
    ke kumu oiaio
ornament—ka-hiko; he mea ka-hiko
other—kela; kekahi; mea aku
otherwise—i ole ia; ka kakou
ought—kupono; mea pono; e pono
our—kakou
ours—ko kakou
ourselves—kakou iho
out—iwaho
outside—mawaho
over—ma o; ma kekahi aoao; aia i o
overcoat—kuka nui
owe—aie
owl—manu pueo
own—nou ponoi
owner—he ona; mea nona ka waiwai
oxygen—ea-mama; (kupono no ke ola kino)
oyster—olepe

P

pace—kikoo wawae
pack—puolo
package—puolo ukana
page—aoao; o ka puke a nupepa
paid—uku aku

pail—pakeke
pain—ehaeha
paint—pena
pair—palua
palace—pa ali
pale—nananakea; haikea
palm—aau loulu; ka poho lima
pan—pakini
pant—naenae; paupauaho
papa—papa
paper—pepa
parcel—he puolo
pardon—huikalaia
parlor—lumi hookipa
part—apana
partly—kekahi apana
party—kekahi poe; anaina ahaaina
pass—maalo; palapala ae; he moali alanui
passage—huakai
passenger—ohua
passion—no ka noonoo weliweli; na noonoo huhu
pasture—pa hookuu holoholona
patch—pahonohono; poho
path—he alahele
patience—hoomanawanui
pattern—a-na
pay—uku
pea—pi
peace—maluhia
peach—piki
pearl—momi
pear—pea
peculiar—ano-e
pen—peni-inika
pencil—penikala
penny—keneka
people—lahuikanaka; makaainana
per—nou iho; owau; hookahi

perceive—hoomaopopo
perfect—hoopono; pololei; maoli
perform—hooko hana
perhaps—anoai; a no ka mea
period—kiko kahi; ka wa o kekahi manawa
perish—o make auanei
person—ke kino; no'u ponoi iho
physician—kauka hoola
pick—ohi; lalau
picture—kii

piece—apana; mahele apana
pillow—uluna
pine—kumulaau paina
pink—akala
pit—lua
pitch—e hoonou; e hoolei; e kiola
place—wahi
plain—kula panoa; maopopo
pan—papahana
plant—mea kanu
play—paani
plead—pale olelo
pleasant—oluolu; kalaelae
please—oluolu
pleasure—oluolu; malio
plot—ohumu kipi; kaha kii o ka aina
plow—palau
pluck—ako
plum—palama; hua meaai
plunge—lele kawa; kimo
poem—mele
point—kumu; oioi; lae
poison—laau make
pond—loko i'a
pony—lio opiopio
poor—ilihune
pop—poka
population—lahui; makaainana

porch—lanai
port—awa kumoku
portion—mahele; kekahi hapa
portly—puipui
position—oihana; kulana
possess—paa ia ana; kuleana
possession—noho mana ana; e paa ana
post—hoonoho; pou; ke kahua
pot—ipu hao; ipu lepo
potato—uala
pound—paona
pour—ninini
powder—pauka
power—mana
practical—hana lima maoli
praise—hoonani
pray—pule
prayer—kanaka hai pule
preach—haiolelo
precious—makamae; hiwahiwa
prefer—e aho
prepare—hoomakaukau
presence—imua o ke alo; hiki kino mai
present—keia manawa; ua hiki mai
preserve—e malama
president—pelekikena
press—kaomi; papapa'i nupepa
pretty—u'i
prevail—lanakila; laha; mau
prevent—ke'ake'a; pale
prey—waiwai pio
price—kumukuai
priest—kahunapule
pride—haaheo; hookiekie; hookano
prince—keikialii
princess—kama'liiwahine
principal—he kumu poo; ke poo
print—pa'i palapala

prison—halepaahao
prisoner—paahao
private—maluhia
prize—makana
probable—anoai; oia paha
problem—nane
proceed—homaka aku
process—kumu hoohana; kekahi ano e hoohana ai
proclaim—kalahea
produce—na mea i hoohua ia mai
product—ka hua loaa
professor—kanaka naauao; kuhikuhi puuone
profit—ka puka
progress—holomua
promise—olelo hoopaa
prompt—hoea mua
pronounce—puana; kukala
proof—hooia; hoike
proper—mea pono
property—waiwai pa
prophet—kaula
proportion—hookaulike
propose—hoike manao; noi; noi e male
prospect—nanaina
protect—kakoo; hoopakela
proud—hookano
prove—hooia; hooiaio
provide—hoolawa
province—panalaau
public—lehulehu
publish—e hoolaha
puff—puahiohio; haanui
pull—huki
pulse—pana
pump—pauma; niele maalea
punish—hoopa'i
punishment—hoopa'i
pupil—haumana

purchase—kuai
pure—oiaio; maemae
purpose—manaopaa
purple—poni
purse—paiki; eke
pursue—hahai; alualu
push—pahu
puss—popoki
put—i waiho aku; kukulu aku; a waiho aku
puzzle—hoohuahualau

Q

quality—ke ano
quantity—ka nui
quarter—hapaha
queen—moiwahine
queer—ano e
question—ninau
quick—awiwi
quiet—maluhia
quit—haalele; waiho; hoopau
quite—pela; aneane

R

rabbit—iole lapaki
race—kukini; mamo
rack—wahi-kau

rag—awelu
rage—keeo; kupikupikio
rail—kaola; alahao
railroad—alahao
rain—ua
raise—hoopiiia; hoomahuahua
ran—ua holo
range—kahi ki-pu ma-ka
rank—kulana iloko o kekahi oihana
rapid—hikiwawe
rare—ike pinepine ole ia; hilu
rat—iole
rather—e aho
ray—kukuna
raw—maka; kolekole
reach—hiki aku
read—heluhelu
ready—makaukau
real—oiaio
really—he oiaio
realm—aupuni nohoalii ia
rear—mahope
reason—ke kumu
receive—loaa mai
recent—ano koke
recognize—hoomaopopo
record—hoopaaia
recover—palekana; loaa hou ke ola
red—ulaula
redhot—enaena
reduce—hoemi
regard—e pili ana; aloha
refuse—hoole
region—kekahi mahele aina
register—puke hoopaa; kakauinoa
regular—maa mau; hana mau
reign—ke au o ka manawa; ka noho mana ana
rejoice—hauoli

72

relate—e pili ana
relation—pilikana
relative—ohana
relief—hoomaha
relieve—maha
religion—hoomana
religious—haipule; manaoio
remain—koena
remember—hoomananao
remove—hooneeia
render—haawi ana aku
rent—hoolimalima
repair—hana hou
repeat—puana hou; hoi palua
reply—pane
report—hoike
reporter—mea kakau hunahuna mea hou no ka nupepa
represent—e ku no ha'i
representative—mea i kohoia
request—noi; nonoi ia mai
require—e koi; he mea pono
reserve—hookoe; malamaia
resolve—hooholoia
respect—mahalo; haawi i ka mahalo
rest—hoomaha
restore—hoihoi hou
result—ka hopena mai
retire—waiho aku
reveal—hoikeia ae
revenge—manao hooko no ka panai i ke ino
review—hoi hope hou; makaikai
reward—makana
rib—iwi aoao
ribbon—lipine
rice—laiki
rid—koe ole; pau loa
rich—waiwai
ride—holo

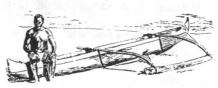

73

ridge—lihiihi
right—pololei; akau
ring—kani; komo
ripe—pala
rise—pii; ala ae
river—kahawai
road—alanui
roar—halulu
roast—hoomo'a
rob—powa
robber—powa
robe—lole hoolu'elu'e
robin—manu
rock—pohaku
rod—kamokoi; laau kukulu a-na aina
rode—ua holo
roll—kakaa
roof—kaupoku
root—aa
rope—kaula
rose—pua loke; ua ala ae
rotten—popopo; palaho
rough—kalakala
round—poepoe
route—alahele
row—laina; haunaele
rub—anai
rubber—laholio
rude—mahaoi
rug—moena pulu
ruin—ilikoli; kahua i helelei; hiolo
rule—lula
ruler—mana hoomalu
run—holo
rush—hoawiwi
rust—popo

S

sable—eleele; pouli
sack—eke; ekeeke
sacred—laahia loa; kapukapu
sacrifice—mohai; kuai hoopoho
sad—kaumaha; luuluu
saddle—noho lio
safe—pakele; pahu hao
safety—maluhia; malu; lulu
said—kamailio; olelo
sail—holo
sailor—kela moku
saint—kekahi mea hemolele
sake—pono
salary—uku paa; uku kumau
sale—kuai
salt—paakai
sand—one
sang—himeni; mele
sat—noho
satisfy—lawa
save—hookoe; koe; malama
saw—ike; pahiolo
say—kamailio; olelo
scale—unahi; paona; pii
scatter—lu helelei
scene—nanaina
scare—maka'u; puiwa; hoemu
scarce—aohe loaa wale
school—kula
science—akeakamai
scold—nuku
score—papa kakau hoopaa hauhelu
scorn—pahenehene; hoowahawaha
scratch—uwa'u; kahakaha
scream—uwa

sea—moanakai
seal—kila
search—imi; huli hele
season—ka manawa; kikina o ka manawa
seat—noho
second—helu elua
secret—mea huna
section—kekahi mahele; apana
secure—e loaa
see—ike
seed—hua
seek—huli; imi
seem—malia
seen—ikeia
seize—hopu aku
seldom—kakaikahi
select—wae; kohoia
self—ia oe iho
sell—kuai aku
send—hoouna
sense—ike; noonoo maikai
sent—hoounaia
sentence—hoopa'i
separate—hookaawale
serious—kuoo
servant—kauwa
serve—lawelawe mai; hookoia
service—manawa haipule; ka hana
set—hookupono; hoonoho
settle—hooponoponoia; noho pono
seven—ehiku
seventh—helu ehiku
seventy—kanahiku
several—lehulehu
severe—oolea
sew—humuhumu
shade—malumalu
shadow—a'ka

shake—hoolululi
shall—pela
shame—hilahila
share—mahele
sharp—oi; kila oi; huhu ino
she—oia; (wahine)
shed—malumalu
sheep—hipa
sheet—apana pepa; he uhi moe
shell—pu-pu; ke iwi o ka papa'i
shelter—wahi malu
shepherd—kahuhipa
shield—pale; palekaua
shine—hulali
ship—moku
shirt—palule
shock—ilihia; eehia; naueue
shoe—kamaa
shone—hoike ae
shoot—ki
shop—hale hana
shore—kahakai
short—pokole
shot—poka
should—e pono
shoulder—poohiwi
shout—uwa
show—hoike
shower—he kuaua naulu; auau wai naulu
shut—pani
sick—ma'i
sickness—oma'ima'i
side—aoao
sigh—kaniuhu
sight—ike lihi
sign—hoailona
silence—maluhia
silent—noho malie

silk—kilika
silver—na mea pili kala
simple—mea ole; hiki wale no
sin—hewa
since—mai ia manawa mai
sincere—oiaio; me ka oiaio
sing—himeni
single—hookahi; pa kahi
sir—ae
sister—kaikuahine
sit—noho
six—eono
sixty—kanaono
size—a-na
skill—ike; naauao; piha ike
skin—ili
skirt—palekoki
sky—lewa
slave—kauwa
sleep—hiamoe
slept—moe; hiamoe
slide—pakika; panee
slight—pa malie
slip—pakika; mu'umu'u
slope—kualapa; ano hi-o
slow—lohi
slumber—hiamoe; hiolani
small—uuku
smart—akamai
smell—aala
smile—minoaka
Smith—Kamika
smoke—uwahi
smooth—pahee; laumania
snap—iloko o ka wa pokole; pana ana o ka lima
snake—moo
snow—hau; noe
so—oia no

soap—kopa
sober—kuoo; he mea ona lama ole
society—he ahahui; he anaina launa
soft—palupalu
soil—lepo; halepolepo
sold—kuai; lilo
soldier—koa
sole—poli wawae; kuakahi
solid—paa; paakiki
some—kekahi
somebody—kekahi poe; kekahi mea e aku
something—kekahi manawa
somewhat—iki; kekahi mea
son—keikikane
song—he mele
soon—kokoke; pokole; manawa ole
sore—eha
sorrow—kaumaha; luuluu
sorry—kaumaha; ehaeha
sort—ke ano
sought—iini; huli
soul—uhane
sound—halulu
soup—kupa
source—kumu; ano
south—komohana
sow—puaa kumulau; lulu hua
space—ka wa
Spain—Kepania
sparkle—hulali
speak—kamailio; olelo
spear—ihe; pono kaua
speech—haiolelo
speed—holonui
special—kuikawa
spell—pela
spend—hoolilo
spin—niniu; kakaa

spirit—uhane
spite—lokoino; hoolohe ole
splendid—nani; kamahao
spoil—inoino; na waiwai pio
spoke—walaau; kamailio
spoon—puna
sport—paani loealea
spot—kahi; kohu
sprang—ua lele
spread—uhola
spring—kupulau; kila holu
spy—kiu
square—kuea; kaulike
stable—hale lio
stain—kohu
stair—anu'u alapii
stamp—poo leka; kuni
stand—ku; pakaukau
standard—kulana
star—hoku
start—hoomaka
starve—pololi
state—hoike
station—wahi hoolulu
statue—kia hoomanao
steal—aihue
steam—mahu
steady—paa mau; hana mau
stay—e noho
steel—kila
steep—kiekie; ku-ho
stem—kumu o ka uwaki; kumukumu laau
step—keehi'na
stick—laau; pipili
stiff—paakiki; oolea
still—maluhia
sting—kikoia
stir—hoonioni; e wili; hoohuihui

80

stock—pu-a
stocking—kakini
stole—ua aihueia
stone—pohaku
stood—ku
stoop—kulou
stop—uoki
store—halekuai
storm—he ino
stormy—inoino
story—moolelo
stout—pu'ipu'i
stove—kapuahi
straight—pololei
strain—kanana; maloeloe
strange—ano-e
stranger—malihini
straw—mauu; opala
stream—kahawai
street—alanui
strength—ikaika
stretch—kikoo; hohola
strike—e hahau
string—kaula
strip—maihi; molina; apanapana loihi
stroke—i ka pa ana
strong—ikaika
struck—ua pa
struggle—aumeume; hakoakoa
student—haumana
study—hoopaanaau
stuff—nui na ano; hoopiha aku
stump—kumukumu
style—hiehie
subject—kumuhana
submit—waiho aku
succeed—hooko
success—holomua

successful—holomua
such—oia ae la
sudden—emoole
suffer—ehaeha
sufficient—ua lawa
sugar—kopaa
suit—paa lole; hoopii kanawai; kupono
sum—huina
summer—kau makalii
summon—kukala; palapala kena
sun—la
sunshine—olino o ka la; puka ka la
superior—he mea kiekie ae; oi ae
supper—ai'na ahiahi
supply—hoolawa
support—malama; e hoolako; kokua
suppose—ina paha
sure—oiaio; pololei
surface—iliwai
surgeon—kauka oki
surprise—puiwa; hikilele
surround—hoopuni
swallow—ua ale; moni
sway—hoomalu ana; luli
sweep—pulumi; kahili
sweet—momona
swell—pehu; o-hu nalu
swift—hikiwawe; awiwi
swim—au
swing—koali
sword—pahikaua
system—he ano e hoonohonoho pono ana

T

table—pakaukau
tail—huelo

tailor—he mea humu lole
take—lawe
tale—moolelo
talk—walaau; kamailio
tall—kiekie
tame—laka
tap—kike
task—ko'iko'i
taste—hoao
taught—a'o aku
tea—ki
teach—a'o
teacher—kumukula
team—paa holoholona hoounauna
tear—uhae; waimaka
teeth—niho
tell—ha'i; hoike
temper—kona inaina
temple—wahi hoomana
tempt—hoowalewale
ten—umi
tend—e kiai; e malama; e nee
tender—haawi; palupalu; waiho aku
tent—hale pe'a; hale lole
tenth—helu umi
terrible—weliweli; kau ka weli
territory—kelikole
terror—hopohopo; maka'uka'u
test—hana hoao
than—ia manawa
thank—mahalo
that—kela
the—ka; ke
theatre—hale keaka
thee—ia oe
their—ko lakou
them—o lakau
themselves—ia lakou iho

then—alaila; ia wa
thence—mai laila aku
there—aia
therefore—a no ka mea
these—keia mau
they—lakou
thick—manoanoa
thief—aihue; mea aihue
thin—lahilahi
thine—o kau
thing—mea
think—noonoo
third—ekolu; helu ekolu
thirst—makewai
thirteen—umikumamakolu
thirty—kanakolu
this—keia
thorn—kuku
thorough—pau pono
those—kela
thou—ia oe; i kou
though—eia nae
thought—noonoo; manao
thousand—kaukani
thread—lopi
threaten—hooweliweli
three—ekolu
throat—a-i
throne—nohoalii
through—pau; pau pono
throw—kiola; hoolei
thrust—e hou aku; e o
thunder—hekili
thus—penei
ticket—kikiki
tide—ke-au
tie—nakinaki
tight—paakiki

till—a hiki
time—manawa
tin—kini
tiny—palanaiki
tip—piko; wekiu; lauolelo; haawi manawalea
tired—luhi
'tis—oia
title—poo manao; kulana hanohano
to—ia
tobacco—paka
today—keia la
toe—manamana wawae
toil—kamau; ahonui; hoomanawanui
told—hoike; kamailio aku
tomorrow—apopo
ton—kana
tone—ke kani ana o ka leo
tongue—alelo
tonight—keia po
too—oia kekahi
took—lawe
tool—mea paahana
tooth—papaniho
top—poo; luna
torn—uhae
toss—kiloiloi
total—huina
touch—hoopa
tower—puo'a
town—kaona
toy—mea paani na na keiki
trace—meheu
track—moali alanui
trade—oihana kalepa;
train—kaaahi
trap—umiki; upiki
travel—makaikai
traveler—mea kahele; makaikai

tread—hehi
treat—lapaau; haawi
tree—kumulaau
tremble—haalulu
trial—hookolokolo
tribe—mamo
trick—maalea
tried—hoaoia
trim—aulii; mikioi
trip—kalepa
troop—pualikoa
trouble—pilikia
true—oiaio
trumpet—o-lea puhi
trunk—pahu lole; kumu laau
trust—hilinai
truth—oiaio
try—hoao
tube—ohe
tumble—hooku'i a hina
tune—ka leo mele
turn—hoohuli; kou manawa
twelve—umikumamalua
twenty—iwakalua
twice—palua
twin—mahoe
two—elua
type—ke ano o kekahi mea; hua kepau hoolaha nupepa

U

ugly—inoino
uncle—makuakane ohana
under—malalo
understand—maopopo
understood—hoomaopopo

unhappy—kaumaha
union—hui
uniform—makalike
unite—hoohuiia
universal—pili laula
university—kula nui
unknown—ike ole ia; aohe ike ia
unless—aia wale no
upright—ku pololei; pololei pu
until—a hiki
unto—a kau aku; maluna
up—iluna
upon—maluna
upper—maluna ae
upward—iluna ae
urge—hookikina
urinate—e mimi
us—kakou
use—pomaikai; waiwai
usual—ano mau
useful—waiwai nui
utter—hoopu-a

V

vain—makehewa; waiwai ole; haakei; hookiekie
valley—awawa
valor—ana koa
valuable—waiwaii'o
value—waiwaii'o
vanish—nalohia
vanity—kilohi; haakei
vapor—mahu; ohu

variety—na ano like ole
various—na mea like ole
vary—loli ae; hoano e
vast—nui hewahewa; palena ole
vegetable—meaai launahelehele
vein—aa koko
velvet—weleweka
verse—pauku
very—ano; maoli
vessel—moku
vest—puliki
veto—hoole
vex—hoonaukiuki
vice—hewa; hala; ino
victory—lanakila
view—nana; nanaina
village—kulana pupupu hale
vine—mala waina
violet—waioleka; pua
virtue—pono; mana
visit—kipa
visitor—makaikai
voice—leo
volume—na aoao o ka puke; punonohu
vote—koho
vow—hoohiki
voyage—huakai hele
vulgar—kuaaina

W

wabble—onioni
wage—ka uku; hoouka
wagon—kaa
waist—ka puhaka
wait—kali

wake—ala
walk—hele
wall—paia
wallet—aa; eke
wander—auwana; kuewa
want—makemake
war—kaua
warm—mehana
warn—kalahea; kukala; a'o
warrior—kanaka koa
was—aia
wash—holoi
waste—uhauha; mauna wale
watch—makaala; uwaki
water—wai
wave—nalu
wax—pilali
way—aoao; ano; ala
we—kakou
weak—palupalu
weakness—nawaliwali; oma'ima'i
wealth—kuonoono
weapon—mea kaua; mea hoeha aku
wear—aahu
weary—luhi; maloeloe
weather—pili i ke ano ino a malie o ke kau
weave—ulana
wee—iki; liilii loa; uuku
weed—nahelehele; waele
week—pule
welcome—hookipa; kipa aloha
well—oluolu; punawai
weep—uwe
weight—ko'iko'i
went—hele
were—aia hoi; ua
west—komohana
western—kukulu komohana

wet—pulu; kawa-u
whale—kohola
what—heaha
whatever—kela ame keia
wheat—huika
wheel—huila
whence—mai hea; ma kahi
whenever—i ka wa; aia a
where—ihea
wherever—ma kahi
which—ka mea hea
while—pela iki
whip—uwepa
whisper—hawanawana
whistle—hopio; oeoe
white—keokeo
who—owai
whole—holookoa
whom—ia wai
whose—kona
why—nokeaha
wicked—hewa; noonoo inoino
wide—akea
width—laula
wife—wahine i male ia
wiggle—laumilo
wild—ahiu; huhu
wilderness—waoakua; waonahele
will—hooilina
willing—aa
win—eo
wind—makani
wine—waina
window—puka aniani
wing—eheu
winter—kau ino o ka makahiki
wipe—holoi loa
wire—uwea

wisdom—naauao
wise—naauao
wish—iini
wit—olelo naauao; noeau
witch—ano akua; kilokilo; hoonohonoho akua
with—me
withdraw—unuhi mai; haalele
within—maloko; maloko mai
without—mea ole; mawaho ae
witness—hoike
woe—popilikia nui; luuluu
wolf—ilio hae
woman—wahine
women—wahine
won—eo
wonder—ha'oha'o; kamahao
wonderful—kupaianaha; u'i
won't—aole
wood—wahie; laau
wooden—laau
wool—huluhulu
word—huaolelo
wore—aahu
world—honua
work—hana
worm—ilo
worn—maluhiluhi; alu'a
worse—lapuwale loa; oi aku
worship—hoomana
worst—ino loa
worth—waiwaii'o kupono
worthy—kupono; pono; hoopono
would—e; oia hoi
wound—palapu
wrap—puolo; uhi; kihei; e opiopi
wreath—lei
wreck—ili
wrestler—mea hakookoo

write—kakau
written—kakauia
wrong—hewa
wrote—kakau
wrought—kalakala; hao i ku'iia

Y

yam—uhi
yard—anana
ye—o oe; oukou
year—makahiki
yearn—iini
yellow—melemele
yelp—aoaoa
yes—ae
yesterday—inehinei
yet—eia nae
yonder—ma o; i o
you—o oe
young—opiopio
your—kou
yourself—ia oe iho
youth—opio

Z

zeal—manoa ikaika
zero—ole
zone—keei

"The Loveliest Fleet of Islands That Lies Anchored in Any Ocean"

"No...land in all the world has any deep, strong charm for me but that one; no other land could so longingly and beseechingly haunt me sleeping and waking, through half a life-time, as that one has done. Other things leave me but it abides; other things change but it remains the same. For me its balmy airs are always blowing, its summer seas flashing in the sun; the pulsing of its surf-beat is in my ear; I can see its garlanded crags; its leaping cascades; its plumy palms drowsing by the shore; its remote summits floating like islands above the cloud rack; I can feel the spirit of its woodland solitudes; I can hear the plash of its brooks; in my nostrils still lives the breath of flowers that perished twenty years ago."

—Mark Twain